DATE: _____

> The secret of getting ahead is getting started.
> MARK TWAIN

The elevator to success is out of order. You'll
have to use the stairs… one step at a time.
JOE GIRARD

I have not failed. I've just found 10,000 ways that won't work.
THOMAS A. EDISON

DATE:

Always do your best. What you plant now, you will harvest later.
OG MANDINO

If you're going through hell keep going.
WINSTON CHURCHILL

A single arrow is easily broken,
but not ten in a bundle.
PROVERB

DATE:

Don't go around saying the world owes you a living.
The world owes you nothing. It was here first.
MARK TWAIN

DATE: _____

All our dreams can come true if we
have the courage to pursue them.
WALT DISNEY

DATE:

Be yourself. Everyone else is taken.
OSCAR WILDE

DATE: _____

The best way out is always through.
ROBERT FROST

I find that when you have a real interest in life and a
curious life, that sleep is not the most important thing.
MARTHA STEWART

DATE:

Innovation distinguishes between a leader and a follower.
STEVE JOBS

You are never too old to set another
goal or to dream a new dream.
C.S. LEWIS

There is no traffic jam along the extra mile.
ROGER STAUBACH

The possibilities are numerous once
we decide to act and not react.
GEORGE BERNARD SHAW

DATE:

Failure is the condiment that gives success its flavor.
TRUMAN CAPOTE

A successful man is one who can lay a firm foundation
with the bricks others have thrown at him.
DAVID BRINKLEY

Act as if what you do makes a difference. It does.
WILLIAM JAMES

DATE:

Little minds are tamed and subdued by misfortune;
but great minds rise above it.
WASHINGTON IRVING

DATE:

What you do today can improve all your tomorrows.
RALPH MARSTON

DATE: _____

DATE: _____

To accomplish great things, we must not only act,
but also dream, not only plan, but also believe.
ANATOLE FRANCE

DATE: _____

Setting goals is the first step in turning
the invisible into the visible.
TONY ROBBINS

Every worthy act is difficult. Ascent is always difficult.
Descent is easy and often slippery.
MAHATMA GANDHI

Just when the caterpillar thought the world
was ending, he turned into a butterfly.
PROVERB

DATE:

Do not wait to strike till the iron is hot;
but make it hot by striking.
WILLIAM BUTLER YEATS

No one can make you feel inferior without your consent.
ELEANOR ROOSEVELT

DATE:

We become what we think about most of the time,
and that's the strangest secret.
EARL NIGHTINGALE

DATE:

I've found that luck is quite predictable. If you want more luck, take more chances. Be more active. Show up more often.
BRIAN TRACY

Be miserable. Or motivate yourself.
Whatever has to be done, it's always your choice.
WAYNE DYER

DATE:

Things work out best for those who make
the best of how things work out.
JOHN WOODEN

If you are not willing to risk the usual you
will have to settle for the ordinary.
JIM ROHN

Do not let what you cannot do interfere with what you can do.
JOHN WOODEN

If you want to make a permanent change, stop focusing on the
size of your problems and start focusing on the size of you!
T. HARV EKER

It is never too late to be what you might have been.
GEORGE ELIOT

DATE:

The only place where success comes
before work is in the dictionary.
VIDAL SASSOON

Learn from the past, set vivid, detailed goals for the future, and live
in the only moment of time over which you have any control: now.
DENIS WAITLEY

I believe that the only courage anybody ever needs
is the courage to follow your own dreams.
OPRAH WINFREY

When I dare to be powerful, to use my strength in the service of
my vision, then it becomes less and less important whether I am afraid.
AUDRE LORDE

Most of the important things in the world have been accomplished by people who have kept on trying when there seemed to be no help at all.
DALE CARNEGIE

DATE: ....

If you don't design your own life plan, chances are you'll fall into some-
one else's plan. And guess what they have planned for you? Not much.
JIM ROHN

DATE: _____

Whenever you see a successful person you only see the
public glories, never the private sacrifices to reach them.
VAIBHAV SHAH

DATE: ....

DATE: _____

Our greatest glory consist not in never falling,
but in rising every time we fall.
OLIVER GOLDSMITH

Whenever you find yourself on the side of the majority,
it is time to pause and reflect.
MARK TWAIN

DATE:

You've got to get up every morning with determination
if you're going to go to bed with satisfaction.
GEORGE LORIMER

DATE: _____

The successful warrior is the average man, with laser-like focus.
BRUCE LEE

DATE:

In order to carry a positive action we must
develop here a positive vision.
DALAI LAMA

Ah, but a man's reach should exceed his grasp,
or what's a heaven for?
ROBERT BROWNING

People often say that motivation doesn't last. Well,
neither does bathing—that's why we recommend it daily.
ZIG ZIGLAR

I often say "pursue excellence, ignore success."
Success is a by-product of excellence.
DEEPAK CHOPRA

The road to success and the road to failure
are almost exactly the same.
COLIN R. DAVIS

What seems to us as bitter trials are often blessings in disguise.
OSCAR WILDE

DATE:

Every great dream begins with a dreamer. Always
remember, you have within you the strength, the patience,
and the passion to reach for the stars to change the world.
HARRIET TUBMAN

DATE:

Try not to become a person of success,
but rather try to become a person of value.
ALBERT EINSTEIN

The only way of finding the limits of the possible is
by going beyond them into the impossible.
ARTHUR C. CLARKE

There are two types of people who will tell you that you
cannot make a difference in this world: those who are
afraid to try and those who are afraid you will succeed.
RAY GOFORTH

Success is the sum of small efforts, repeated day in and day out.
ROBERT COLLIER

All progress takes place outside the comfort zone.
MICHAEL JOHN BOBAK

All life is an experiment. The more
experiments you make, the better.
RALPH WALDO EMERSON

DATE: _____

The function of leadership is to produce
more leaders, not more followers.
RALPH NADER

When you stop chasing the wrong things,
you give the right things a chance to catch you.
LOLLY DASKAL

To dare is to lose one's footing momentarily.
Not to dare is to lose oneself.
SØREN KIERKEGAARD

Success is the sum of small efforts,
repeated day-in and day-out.
ROBERT COLLIER

DATE:

You measure the size of the accomplishment by the
obstacles you had to overcome to reach your goals.
BOOKER T. WASHINGTON

The number one reason people fail in life is because
they listen to their friends, family, and neighbors.
NAPOLEON HILL

Sooner or later, those who win are those who think they can.
RICHARD BACH

DATE:

As we look ahead into the next century,
leaders will be those who empower others.
BILL GATES

Too many of us are not living our dreams
because we are living our fears.
LES BROWN

Every noble work is at first impossible.
THOMAS CARLYLE

If you want to achieve excellence, you can get there today.
As of this second, quit doing less-than-excellent work.
THOMAS J. WATSON

The great thing in this world is not so much
where you stand, as in what direction you are moving.
OLIVER WENDELL HOLMES

DATE: _____

Life is not about finding yourself. Life is about creating yourself.
LOLLY DASKAL

Great minds discuss ideas; average minds discuss events;
small minds discuss people.
ELEANOR ROOSEVELT

DATE:

It's not whether you get knocked down; it's whether you get up.
VINCE LOMBARDI

DATE:

Success is walking from failure to failure
with no loss of enthusiasm.
WINSTON CHURCHILL

DATE: _____

It is possible to live happily in the here and now. So many conditions
of happiness are available—more than enough for you to be happy
right now. You don't have to run into the future in order to get more.
THICH NHAT HANH